ONCE UPON A TIME IN

THE
MIRACLE
DOCTOR

JILLIAN LIN
Illustrations by SHI MENG

*Hua Tuo (around AD 200),
doctor/healer, Eastern Han Dynasty*

Once upon a time in China...

… lived a boy called Hua (*Wah*). His father died when he was seven, and Hua grew up very poor. He was lucky if he had a spoonful of rice to eat for the day, and his dirty clothes were full of holes. The people around him were also poor. Many had fallen ill from diseases and not having enough to eat.

His mother said, 'Son, you'd better study hard so you'll find a good job. Then we won't have to suffer any longer.'

Hua thought for a while and said, 'I've seen many people around us fall ill. I wish I could have done something to help them. That is why I want to become a doctor.'

At once, Hua's mother sent a letter

to a famous doctor called Dr. Cai (*Tsai*). She asked

if he could teach her son everything about medicine.

The doctor agreed to see Hua, but only because he

had once been close friends with Hua's father.

Hua walked hundreds of miles to see Dr. Cai. When he finally arrived, he saw the doctor's students picking leaves from a mulberry tree. They had trouble reaching the leaves on top of the tree.

Dr. Cai decided to test Hua and asked, 'Can you think of a way to pick the leaves from the highest branch of that tree?'

'No problem,' said Hua. 'I just need a piece of rope.'

He tied one end of the rope to a small rock and threw the rope over the highest branch of the tree.

The weight of the rock made the branch bend, and Hua easily pulled the leaves from the branch.

Dr. Cai nodded. 'Very good. But I wonder if you can solve this problem.' He pointed at two goats who were

locking horns as they were fighting in the courtyard. No matter how hard Dr. Cai's students tried, they could not pull them apart.

Smiling, Hua said, 'I'll give it a try.'

He turned on his heel and went out into the fields to pick two big handfuls of grass. He placed one bunch a few steps away from one goat and the other next to the second goat.

Within seconds, the goats stopped fighting. They turned up their noses to smell the fresh grass and started munching away.

Dr. Cai and his students clapped their hands.

'Excellent,' said Dr. Cai. 'From now on, I will teach you everything I know.'

As Dr. Cai's student, Hua worked very hard. He learned to use different plants as medicine. He also learned to treat sick people by pricking thin needles into their bodies. This is called acupuncture, and it is still used today.

After a few years, Hua went into the world to put into practice what he had learned. He treated and cured many people using herbs and acupuncture. If that didn't work, he performed operations on them by cutting into their bodies.

Hua was the first person in history to invent a drink that puts people into a kind of sleep. That way they would not feel pain during surgery.

After treating many patients, Hua often wondered why people fell ill and how he could help them. He came up with an idea.

'To stay healthy, you must do exercise,' he told his patients. 'Copy the movements of animals like the deer, bird, tiger, bear, and monkey. When you do these exercises, you will be ill less often.'

Hua wrote all his findings in books and became famous. People called him 'The Miracle Doctor'.

One day, a powerful army leader called Cao Cao (*Tsow Tsow*) asked to see him. By then, Hua was nearly a hundred years old, but he still looked young and healthy.

'Dr. Hua, I am suffering from terrible headaches,' Cao Cao said.

'I will treat you with acupuncture, Sir.' Hua pricked needles on Cao Cao's head, neck, arms, and legs. Soon, Cao Cao felt much better and asked him to become his personal doctor.

Each time Cao Cao had a headache, Hua came running to treat him.

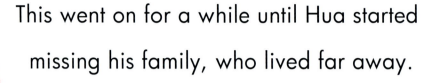

This went on for a while until Hua started missing his family, who lived far away. Hua wanted to go home, but he knew Cao Cao would get angry with him, so he told him a lie.

'My wife has fallen ill. I'll have to go home, Sir.'

Cao Cao was not happy to hear this, but he let him go.

Of course, Hua was overjoyed to go back to his old life. But it wasn't long before he received letters from Cao Cao asking him to come back. Hua wrote back to him using the excuse that his wife was still unwell.

When Cao Cao had a really bad headache one day, he asked his servants to spy on Hua.

'If his wife is really ill,' he told them, 'give him these silver coins. But if he's lying, throw him in prison right away.'

The servants went to his village and found out that Hua had lied. They immediately grabbed him and locked him up in prison.

In the last days of his life, Hua was thinking how he could pass on all his knowledge.

He called in the prison guard and told him, 'Please take these books that I've written. They will help save people's lives.'

The guard shook his head. 'I'm sorry, Doctor. I'm scared. If Master Cao finds out, he'll kill me.'

Hua let out a deep sigh. 'Please give me a light.'

The guard did, and Hua set fire
to his books. From that moment on,
his knowledge was lost forever.

Thankfully, people still remember Hua today.

Around the world, they use his animal exercises to stay healthy. In China, they use his name to advertise Chinese medical products like plasters and needles. Some acupuncture points on the spine are also named after him.

Even though it is thousands of years later, Hua is still helping people to stay healthy. And that is why he truly deserves to be called 'The Miracle Doctor'.

1 ~ Hua was fond of reading when he was a child. He devoured all the books he could get his hands on, but was most interested in books about medicine, herbs, and well-known doctors. Inspired by what he had read, he used to  climb the nearby mountains in search of herbs. He used these to treat sick people around him.

2 ~ When a doctor in ancient China proved to be especially skillful, he received a special signboard saying he was a 'Second Hua Tuo'. That shows how much people used to admire Hua.

3 ~ There are 34 acupuncture points on both sides of the human spine that are named after Hua. According to one story, he used these points to heal a man who had problems with his feet and couldn't walk. Hua treated him using the acupuncture points on his back. Soon after the treatment, the man could walk again.

4 ~ The drink Hua had invented to put patients to sleep before he operated on them was a mixture of wine and herbs. It was more than 1,600 years later before Western doctors invented a similar drug to prepare patients for surgery.

5 ~ In many Chinese temples you can find a statue of Hua. People worship him as the God of Medicine and an Immortal (someone who lives forever and never dies).

6 ~ Hua appeared as a character in one of the most famous books in China called *The Romance of the Three Kingdoms*. In it, he treats an army general whose arm was pierced by a poisoned arrow during a battle. Hua performed surgery on him by cutting away flesh and scraping poison from the bone. Meanwhile, the general calmly sat playing a board game.

Even though this is probably a made-up story, some parts of it are true. In the book, the general offered the miracle doctor 100 ounces (about 6.5lb or 3kg) of gold, but Hua refused. He said that a doctor must cure patients, not make money out of them. This is what Hua used to say in real life.

7 ~ Some people believe Cao Cao was angry with Hua for another reason. They say Hua had told him, 'The only way to cure your headaches is for me to cut open your skull and operate on your brain.' When Cao Cao heard this, he got so mad that he threw Hua in prison and ordered his death. No one knows which story is true, but what we do know is that Hua spent the last days of his life locked up, and that all his books were destroyed.

8 ~ The animal exercises Hua invented are also known as the 'Five Animal Play'. They are part of *qigong*, a Chinese exercise program of slow movements and special ways of breathing. Hua believed people should not sit still too much, but keep on moving their bodies. This would improve their flow of blood and energy, and stop them from falling ill.

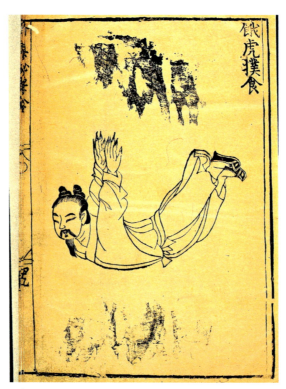

The exercise 'Hungry tiger pounces on its food'.

9 ~ After Hua's death, doctors stopped performing operations. At the time, people believed the body was special. That is why they were against cutting into the body for surgery, even if it would cure a disease.

10 ~ Not long after Hua was put to death, Cao Cao's favorite son fell ill and died. When that happened, Cao Cao sank down on his knees and cried, 'I should never have sentenced Hua to death. He could have saved my son!'

1   When Hua was a boy, why did he want to become a doctor?

a)   Because he wanted to earn lots of money.

b)   Because he wanted to become famous.

c)   Because he wanted to help people who were sick.

2   Why did Dr. Cai agree to take Hua on as his student?

a)   Because Hua was the son of his close friend and he felt sorry for him.

b)   Because Hua showed him he was clever.

c)   Because he wanted to charge him money to study with him.

3   What treatment did Hua give his patients to cure them?

a)   He gave them herbs and pricked thin needles into their skin.

b)   He cut into their bodies.

c)   All of the above.

4 **What did Hua come up with to prevent illness and make people healthier?**

a)   A set of exercises that copy the movements of animals.

b)   A treatment where needles are pricked into your skin.

c)   A special drink that made you feel sleepy.

5 **Why did the army leader Cao Cao put Hua to death?**

a)   Because Hua hurt Cao Cao by pricking his acupuncture needles in the wrong places.

b)   Because Hua did not want to be Cao Cao's personal doctor any longer and told him lies about having to go home.

c)   Because he discovered that Hua had tried to kill him.

Answers to the Quiz: 1. c / 2. b / 3. c / 4. a / 5. b

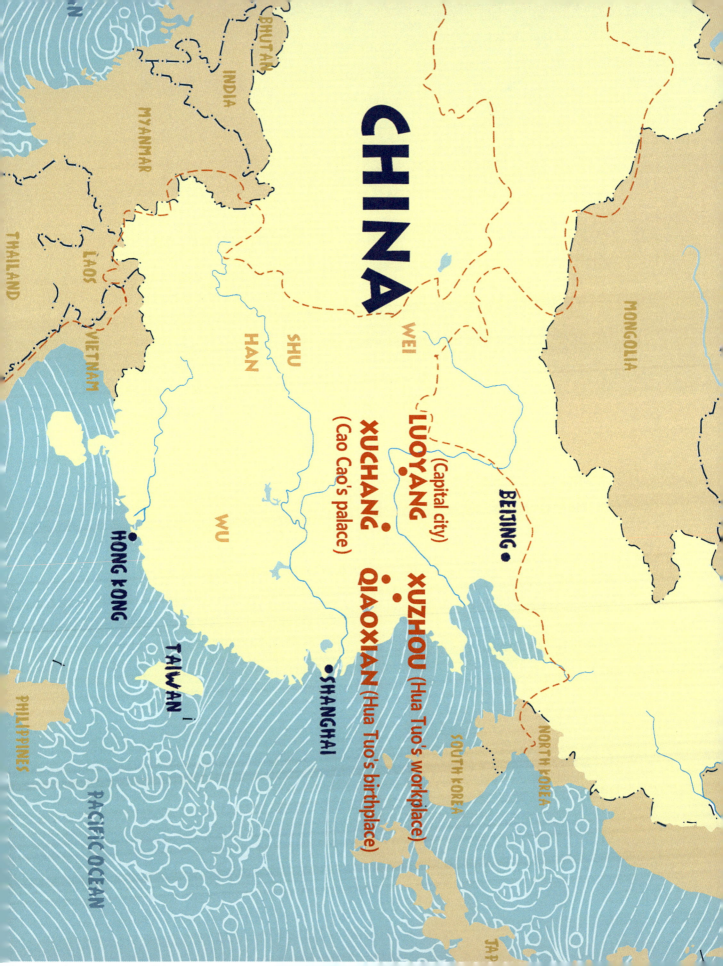

The *Once Upon A Time In China...* Series

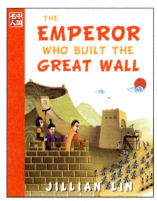
Qin Shihuang

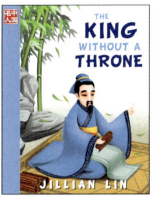
Confucius

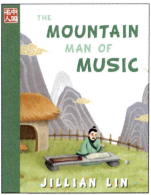
Zhu Zaiyu

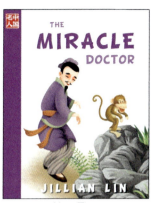
Hua Tuo

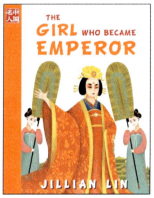
Wu Zetian

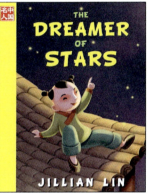
Zhang Heng

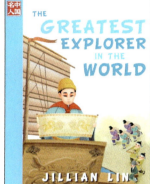
Zheng He

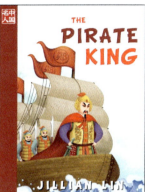
Koxinga

Also available as e-books. For more information, visit

www.jillianlin.com

Made in the USA
Middletown, DE
31 January 2022

60120126R00020